Elegant, cosmic, estranging, wild. In Julia Anna *Long Exposure*, we are both outside and inside, simultaneously internalizing the obsessive mind of a brilliant thinker, but also transforming along a winter highway, a swallowing lake, a hotel room on Earth. Morrison both alarms and enchants with her ability to make disassociating vivid. She never is where she really is, her mind and fantasy structures always wandering, escaping, time traveling. This is a poetic master class in disembodiment, all the while talking about scenes of domesticity and claustrophobic intimacies. It upsets the reader—as in, it will reorient you entirely. Brilliant.

—Megan Fernandes, author of *I Do Everything I'm Told*

This book contains a mesmerizing intimacy unlike anything I've ever read. With extraordinary lyricism, Julia Anna Morrison takes us into landscapes, histories, and moments that open and deepen endlessly, where time blooms and folds and "it starts to snow the / same snow from an unusually painful winter a million years ago." There is a splendor and a candor to these poems that leaves me awestruck. Julia Anna Morrison is a visionary poet, and *Long Exposure* is a completely stunning debut.

—Chloe Honum, author of *The Lantern Room*

Reading Julia Anna Morrison is like reading poems written by wildflowers in the dead of night, buried in snow. With feverish precision and deep magic, Morrison's *Long Exposure* sings the most inconsolable and gorgeous lullaby I've ever heard.

—Sabrina Orah Mark, author of
Happily: A Personal History—with Fairy Tales

As fierce as it is tender, *Long Exposure* performs domestic sorcery. An Ovid of the interior, Morrison invites the subliminal to emerge sublime. The comings and goings of motherhood become as elemental as snow or light or consciousness, as enchanting as a storm or shadow or unconditional love passing across generations. In this otherworldly debut, childhoods bleed like seasons, and the longings of grief and eros transform the lived-in landscape. Rather than capturing a moment, Morrison frees the moment to move, to drift with us and against us: "We go back and forth. We halve each other." *Long Exposure* will not leave you whole or healed; it will multiply you. Lucky us to be guests in Morrison's universe, where "If you are missing, you exist."

—Elizabeth Metzger, author of *Lying In*

While the shutter of Julia Anna Morrison's lens stays open, three decisive figures wander the frame, each becoming a blur within the others and herself: a brother lost in childhood, a lover who didn't stay, and the newborn son who focuses her ardent tenderness. Set in lackluster America, between shaken snow globe Iowa and lakeside Southern fields, this debut is often awake all night, claustrophobic and felt from afar, agitated by sex and boredom, by "desires I am not ready for." Through anxiety and dream, nostalgia, hope, the poet joins her dead sibling's hand to the hand of her "evergreen" boy. Morrison can be self-lacerating, obsessive, or matter-of-fact. Or plangent or soft, even fragile, saying her long goodbyes. "If it didn't get killed in winter," she avers, "it comes back with / color." These are human poems, the kind that bleed.

—Andrew Zawacki, author of *Unsun*

LONG EXPOSURE

poems

Julia Anna Morrison

moon city press
Department of English
Missouri State University

MOON CITY PRESS
Department of English
Missouri State University
901 South National Avenue
Springfield, Missouri 65897

First Edition
Published by Moon City Press, Springfield, Missouri, USA, in
2023.

Library of Congress Cataloging-in-Publication Data

Morrison, Julia Anna.
Long Exposure

Library of Congress Control Number: 2023949046

Further Library of Congress information is available upon request.

ISBN-10: 0-913785-75-X
ISBN-13: 978-0-913785-75-1

Text edited by Karen Craigo
Interior designed by Cam Steilen
Cover designed by Shen Chen Hsieh

Manufactured in the United States of America

www.moon-city-press.com

moon city press
Department of English
Missouri State University

CONTENTS

For my brother, Will,
my son, Félix

and for Catherine

ice ages exist, ice ages exist

—Inger Christensen

I swam
to the surface, like a black, dark-blue
luminous blossom. It's terrible to be
a flower. The world stopped.
Mute, like velvet, I opened, perhaps
for good.

—Tomaž Šalamun

LONG EXPOSURE

poems

MYTHS ABOUT TREES

I would walk across refrigerator water with you
To the other side. I would build a blue kitchen
And flower in it, a single bud. I would burst—
Have our colt over again so you could hum
To it. I would love you only just enough through
The steep Iowa winter. You would barely notice
How cold we were getting. I would cut down the wood to
Find your ship. But there are no trees left in my childhood;
I tore them down looking for my brother when asking
Got me nowhere. And I loved trees. They were all I
Could write about. The only place my thrush would sleep.
I would want to find out we were having a boy, gently this time,
And I would bring you peace.
I don't know if I can do this again, with anyone. It isn't fair
To show them how I was brought here, against my will.
Our son has your eyes, my mouth. Out of my mouth
He says he sees you. I was sure he would look at us
And see who hurt who. That used to be a door.
No, I do not understand when you speak to me. I do not
Know the easy way through this landscape. I don't know why
I live here. And I have lived here so long, most of my
Time. You are a ghost. I do not know how we ever made love,
Or if we did.

PART I

FERTILE WINDOW

TREATMENT

The night you get here, the Earth seems strange,
unmarried, out looking for a mate.

On the fifth floor of the mansion, my eyes close so
the moonflower opens in the peach-colored night.

An anesthesiologist tricks me to sleep. Below us,
rain paints the doors shut-white. I notice

my hands have begun to wrinkle. I hope the Earth finds a
    match
before it gets too old, run over by storms.

My night person carries our baby in his arms. Suddenly,
I am very bored but I am crying. The desire to kiss takes
    me over.
Someone's unbuckled my arms.

I wait for treatment but the doctors are so busy with their
    cloths, their staples.
I don't want to be consoled with a coat.

I am a garden at the dead of winter.

DOES MONOGAMY SUIT YOU

Rain through everything:

Fall goes slowly this year but I do not have time
to remember my life.

Recently I dreamed my own son was small again.

This is how much time has passed.

I am making a film. I film every day,
ten or so seconds, whatever I have to spare.

Tonight, the moon falls out of the frame.

I feel my husband watching me at the window.

I am late for dinner, distracted by evergreens
and plot holes in my life.

One, in particular, whose details have gone missing,
I stare into.

Recordings I refuse to delete clutter my phone:
every snow and what we did with that snow.

My husband takes off his shirt when he comes to bed.

Come out of your shell, my mother always said before I
went to school.

I wear it like a housedress, a nightgown.

In the bed, water pours down my face.
I am clean and unmarried,
still child enough to carry a child,
to be transformed by another bleeding thing.

OFFSPRING

Off the winter highway, years later,
I apologize.

I had something to do with the separation
when you were a baby.

Filling the car with gas four hours from home.

I've forgotten for what exactly, but I am sorry.

You smile at me from the backseat window.
It's cold here and my hands are frozen.

Your father in one world, your mother in another.
Your shoe in one house, your sock in the other.

All of that dreaming in two beds.

We go back and forth. We halve each other.

No wonder we believe so fiercely in magic and
weather. I teach you spells to reach me when I am
not there.

You are doing the disappearing children do—
off to school in your coat, or sleeping with the light off.

My stomach sounds like a phone ringing.
You've left your toy at your father's house.

We arrive to get it, almost immediately.

We enter the room and stand there together.

Will half of me always want to stay here.
Will half of me always want to go.

VISITOR

Barely a splash made the river wider, barely an inflection, a
gash in the covers

Barely a wave in the painting of the ocean,
a blue washed over, a thumb in your lover

Barely a stitch loose in the sock, a handstand, a
sliver of iceberg, barely a lower than

Barely a song in your mouth, barely a bird making of a
bristle, a tooth to brush, barely a promise of a fairy

Barely a montage of a marriage, flickering, a moon painted
onto the sheets. *God is the breath you*—

Barely a depression, a star drooping, the
kettle of peppermint boiling

Barely a peach, barely miscarried on that mattress,
barely home, but home now, sledding

DRIFT

I had a feeling I was married, that we'd signed the
papers and swam in the lake.

I have no photographs of you. But I know your phone
number, that you were born without a cherry.

The kale you grew you didn't eat. It started as an image of
a seed, and then a seedling, something to save our
marriage, though we weren't married.

If you want to get to heaven, which you don't,
you will have to quarantine fourteen days.

You will have to grow weeds and scan your brain for
mildew, rot, the plans to your treehouse.

I found a map to a city & knew I'd lived there, not when,
    but that I
had a tree where I would read. I took baths and a train to
    and from
the city center, a baguette crumbling in my arm.

What's the end point of a marriage, of a husband?
Someone to eat oatmeal with every morning.
Someone to watch your body as you watch your body.

I could only half-raise, half-mother, half-watch the tornado
skidding into the valley.

I wanted to swallow the lake
before it got to me so I could
drift in it.

DEATH BY LANDSCAPE

Wires stick out of my dream & I am plugged in, near the
    water.
A black & white ocean heads for us in the living room. I
    ignore it.

My tan is fading; It's always night here, & I am always
    pregnant,
disappointing you.

It's salt-raining in your big, blank house. The ceilings are
    made of paper,
cracked, about to fall in on us.

There's a baby room, filled with plays.

I picture your death, hang it on the mantle.

I'm distracted by it, like a bad movie.

God is a cliff I never walked off.
I never let anyone hold the full weight of me.

But you lift my arms & crack my back, air bubble by air
    bubble.

We eat dinner, skip the lovemaking, & fall asleep in
    various rooms
of the house, hour to hour until it's morning.

I wanted this poem to start with wires & end with sex,
but I was born in a hospital.

When I was a child, my family ate together at a maple
table until we didn't. We slept on the floor in tired down
comforters.

Half of the children inherited a gift for painting terrifying
objects. The other half guessed what was in them.

This was another world, luckily.
Now it is covered by godawful trees.

DISPATCH

I lived on eggshells once, with my lover.
I ate eggs for every meal.
Listen, the lake keeps chipping into white glass.
I do my best, but I hate spring. It asks too many
questions. We are ordered to stay home and look at
flowers. I am sick of blossoming into a mother. Sick
of wondering if I will ever have another child. At
night, finally. The egglike moon always itself, if
invisible. I sleep in these clothes. I am a museum of
dried roses. Each winter my child eats icicles and
doesn't catch a fever. I can't believe it.
I've been screaming again, like it's perfectly normal.
I stare at the crocuses for an hour, as encouraged.
I wash my fingernails. I feel holy when I vow to love
unconditionally, in a quiet tone of voice, at all times.

AT SQUIRE POINT

I remember I have a child, vaguely.
He wears a raincoat, tiny pine trees on his sailor shoes.

I will have to give him away, very slowly
when winter comes. First one night a week, and then two.

Stars on one ceiling: fishes on another.

Papa is asleep, I say.
I will always want to touch you, I said when he left me.

It won't happen all at once, he said.

First the closets of his winter coats. I braced myself.
It's a million little things: his skin, the tongues of his shoes.

I should have never given birth. I feel a color
he left in my stomach when I am alone, shovel mark.

At quiet hour I hear his papa and me talking before he was born.
Our childless voices, our love over the water.

But these woods are made of dry paper;
I was right; I could not give birth without losing.

Now he asks if I will be his mama
for all of the time,

if those are leaves falling down off my orange shirt. God,

what blankets will I choose for his second bed.
Are the trees against the windows safe.

Once I lost my glove in a city. Somehow it matters
then that I was in love and this had never happened.

HAMMERHEAD

That I wrote anything was a miracle. That I fell in love.
Trees explain, turning away.

Light surprised us both in the middle of our last fight.
We were in a kitchen. With my eyes I covered myself in
 every yellow leaf.

As I get older, I am surprised my heart is muscle, not plant.
The moon is the only model I have for motherhood.

I have known him a few months when a stranger says:
Let's fall asleep and make love in the morning.

I barely sleep, wondering what making love will feel like, if
it's the difference between sleeping and dreaming.

Turns out, I had a son instead.

But on dark nights, I still confuse the room I sleep with my
childhood room: flimsy, blue curtains, all those thick trees out
the window, freed by time, as if to say I can hold your
childhood, and the childhoods before you.

Here it is always fall and your mother is a
sad mother, sewing costumes.

I put on my hood and stand in the rain and the paint won't
 come off.

I remember someone painted a hammerhead on this wall.
I will marry the wrong person, I know, in the dead of night.

There is no difference between making love and dreaming.

ALOUETTE

I died for a long time. Tiny pests grew along
the staircase in my sloping heart.

To myself I said I wanted to be a mother all the time,
a dead green-eyed mother.

Those years next to you I did a lot of wild-flowering
through the drainpipe in my head—

water got in through the storm windows:
At night the rain talked while we slept and didn't disappear.

I showed you the flowers when they were too small to hold. You said
I should leave the house more; ride my blue bike down the hill, rake
the yellow leaves.

I baked a birthday cake, covered it in piles of sugared roses. I am
not happy. Our planet has miles of a moon. I saw me under it,
asking it questions, holding a foldable basket.

I made a child on my own. My first task was to let him be
    born, then
give him as many horses as I could feed.

UNIVERSITY OF IOWA HOSPITALS & CLINICS

I am computer paper. I wish for a pink wedding fleur.

I hear us making love; he got me so pregnant in
a hotel room on Earth.

Horses rose at dawn. I lose my
gloves, dye my hair dark brown.

I throw up on the highway.

One early evening I turn into a mother next
to some rocks and a pond.

When I am alone again, I look at my body:
a stretched-out image of a maiden.

I wonder if I'm sick. I see an evil spot in my eye.

I cover the house in milk and play the rain and the raining.

SUGAR

The winter moon turns on again. I want to lick ice
off the windowpanes.

I haven't left the house today. On this bed I will
become a mother, a cannibal in a wet bra,
eating my placenta like a sugar cube.

Soon my stomachs will empty their baskets of stars
on the ceiling. How hungry will I get.

Every flutter I only imagined the baby an
angel going back to being an angel—born
from the defrosted sea in a bright blue coat.

KATARINA

The pitch pine that used to be a broodmare blows into
   paper, into
the baby-soiled water.

A star charges the twilit pond without fire.

Not ever so sorry am I. Not ever, for being a mother.
I swim four-legged here, my breasts the heavier, the redder.

At night they glow horsey blood. They are for you to see at
   any hour.

For you I ring the bell in the mare until it breaks. For you I
ring the bell sharp in my heart until you know it's me.

AT THE LAKE

The storm sprains the conifers against the
cabin. From the bed, I hear sorrow-boxes
crack open into the lake. Underneath as
many blankets as rose petals, you float by a
thin cord. No wonder. I eat more sullen
flowers to keep your wings from drying.
Won't you blot through my bathing suit.
When you learn to swim, I will take you
down to the water myself and drop you in.

OWL

We are afraid of sex now. I no longer offer
myself to you in the morning because there
is no morning, no body to offer.

And you do not trust me
to take my pills.

I've forgotten what to do when I am alone.

I carry water in a glass cup. I think of ways
to kill the owl, ways to make myself come,
but don't.

I peek at the baby and wish he'd start crying.
I could make him stop.

THE FIELD

You cry at the wooden moon hanging from the sky.
Under your eyelids, an ocean foggy and endless—I swim it
    in the dark.

You are old enough to remember the last world, your last
    mother.

She is mourning you somewhere near Earth, with nothing
    to comfort her but
your fingernails.

Outside, you're blonder than rain. You show me the smallest
    piece of the field before you
swallow it.

You slowly learn to speak to the moon, speak to the animal,
    speak
goodbye—to sleep all night holding nothing.

Years later I feel you kick my stomach with your flower feet.
    The house is empty, only
the rain is starting.

I've choked on everything in the field. I feel you kicking, but
    you are
not there—just the dull scar I couldn't heal—if you were,

I would have you again and again to eat your first glassy tear.

THE MIDDLE HOUSE

Mornings we walk to the edge of the island and it starts to snow

The cells you left in my brain fall around like shaved ice,
a song my mother sang in pieces

I still haven't decided if I will leave you

Winter doesn't give up—it lengthens darkness, your
legs grow up against it

The ice glitters in my sleep, showering so hard I cannot wake

On the day we are supposed to leave the island,
I wait for a cry to come out of a hole in the ice

We run from the hospital each morning and it starts to snow the
same snow from an unusually painful winter a million years ago

SKETCH OF WINTER

I.
In the orchard, snow falls apart. Winter didn't work. Now I
must process green flowers as they happen.

In under an hour, the yard was mostly moon.
The day got so flimsy; it was made of frost paper.

I used the well to disappear in.
I wanted to be like rain slinging. Maybe it is still winter.

II.
That's you on a wooden sled, gliding through the pines on a
Christmas long ago.

Your teeth were deciduous—they fell into my hands at
    nightfall.
You didn't make a peep when I pulled at the root. You
    listened. They
clicked out.

I look for the missing one in the well.

No one will know I am your mother but you do.

I want to carry you away from this night, the dark so slack the
stars go through.

I want to show you the evergreens, how
lenient, how they stay put, even when you take them with you.

SLEEP ANXIETY

Moon violets rush spring. Then bloom the bulbs,
the cherry cutlets.

My son stands in the woods and I crouch
just until I cannot see him: blond hair, yellow raincoat,
six bottom teeth.

Every ginkgo leaf drops the same time to
my feet.

My mother lost her son in these trees. He didn't use
the house key in his pocket because he was not alive.

She washed her black hair and disappeared to dry
hyacinth and some hostas in the yard.

I had to be careful of what she saw, especially at night.

I took her a white blanket the size of the yard, told
her her Will was in heaven

even though he was the blanket she would wrap herself in.
He was the house in the ground, and I was her grief I
    could not see.

My son was mine.

EGGS AFTER SELL-BY DATE

I am the mother here. I sew buttons on coats, match socks.
I peel eggs, chart good behavior, smell your evergreen.

I can tell it snowed last night because we sleep in,
sprinkled with fairy dust, later than usual.

I can tell you it's winter, that my son is four, that I didn't
    scream last night.

White curtain like swordfish, like let me name all the sharks
    I know.

Not now, don't name them now:
goblin shark, sawtooth, lemon, spinner, reef.

I open the white curtain, no surprise.

Snow is a feeling. I can get out of bed, unlike my mother.
I get out of bed every day.

Are you done growing, my son asks.
No, I wink, not even close.

☾

One day I will find a gray hair on my sweater, and it will be
    mine.

For now we stumble into our snowclothes & into the
    sunlight.
I barely look for a trap door, for a stop sign to run.

You are a monster, he says later, after I scream at him for
    not staying in his bed.

He is already bigger than me if I squint my eyes, gentler.

I loosen & hold him in my arms. I remember where I
    parked my
car, next to the snow pile, next to the green hatchback.

My throat is sore, like I've been sledding.
Kissing is still the last thing you have to do.

My son is my fault, my vault of treasure, nothing alike.

He finally sees me the way I ask to be seen, my ugliest:
sick, and not sick of stars.

PART II

MONTAGE OF A DROWNING

MOTHER SUMMER

I am almost eight I can touch
the tops of the cupboard
my teeth half fallen out
half grown in like a meal
I will eat and eat the rest of my life
cereal at night in the blue-dark light
next to the bathtub where my toothbrush
drips like a faucet next to the faucet

I get a green coat on sale that touches
the floor edges the snow-covered road
from my house to someone else's
my son is not home tonight and I am alone
the bathtub is even empty I haven't killed a spider
in a very long time I think another family lives here
when I don't when my son sleeps at his dad's
he sends me his dreams on a piece of paper
I open it in the morning with the curtains
he's dreamed of me again and I can't watch it

summer and I am six in the snow out the window
my dad holds the video camera carves wood into
sounds sleeps next to my mother who is
miscarrying in the red dark she bathes us the next day
the good kind of bubbles I like when she wraps me in a
      towel when she lets
me peel my own nails when she answers the phone
in the bathtub the cord twisted around her wrist
her gold shell earrings her white reeboks her garden shoes

by the front door she's always in the yard these days
making the garden do something for summer for spring

she sleeps in a white blanket in the yard when my brother
goes crazy and dies she sleeps under the very old trees
though she is very young younger than I could ever imagine
I come home to a clean house to a clean brother
after he's gone the kitchen is always dirty and
we don't know what to do with his clothes
it starts to melt in the dead of Christmas
we wear tank tops and skirts and make a boat
from bark and leaves

INVITATION FROM MY BROTHER

Because I was so twisted, I almost killed myself, he writes to me.
   Please come to my baptism.

One night he woke up crying and shook until morning.
   Something about
the devil. As he got older, he started to look like our dead
   brother; even
his voice could trick me.

When he submerged underwater in the church where he
   was born, I stood up.

That was my little brother in a bathtub a million years ago,
   that's who I
used to wake up in the morning.

His love the glimpse of light under a door of a dark night
   he won't get through, but does.

After he came up for air, I never could ask the details of his
   escape plan,
only if the water was warm and chlorinated, if he felt found.

A DISEASE OF THE MIND

Every drip startles me: rain falling off the edge of moon into
    the Earth.

Asleep next to a man who does not love me any more than
    he loves a river.
I move to another room, closer to the rain without being
    touched.

My little brother sleeps (does he sleep?) in a rehab center in
    the Blue Ridge
Mountains. I pray for him to not take his own life. I pray for
    beauty to snap him
out of himself.

When I hear his voice, I know his disease is my fault.
I could have taken it from him under a breath of silver
    stars when he was seven.

It barely fit into his hands it was so small
and oddly complicated, a nightmare. I glimpsed and he shut
    his fingers quickly—

his eyes always so I could never read—high or low—the blue
of them.

The nightmare got stronger, darker, he started having it
    every night.
By then, he'd torn everything off his walls

so the room was blank, so no images touched his sleep.
The blue pills got out of hand. He dug for them in the
    backyard, he shattered

the kitchen glass by glass. I tracked his breathing all night.
    Beauty never snapped me out
of anything for very long. Rain, however.

I have a disease in my mind, he tells me. I don't remember
    when it began.

But I do. The moon is a smudge-light, dulling the backyard
    where my brother and I were
born, not even one after the other, next to the river I love
    him much more than.

VIDEO FOOTAGE

I pack a suitcase to get through October and drive to the
shore with a video camera

It takes years to get anywhere now that I am a mother

I open the camera and listen to my older brother
running to the ocean over the wind
rumbling the microphone

For as long as I knew him, he smelled like
salt water, on his way into the blowing waves

My brother didn't grow old. The sea disappeared
him; the freckle on his earlobe has now appeared
on my ankle

I've stared at that freckle so long I've turned into a
woman who couldn't, after all, when it came down to it,
give up her son

IN PROPORTION

In this study I am allergic
to the ocean
in which my brother
drowned
at his performance,
though I'm much younger
in the inflected and
inflected saline water
No froth in the trachea;
he was not once found
dead. I could have been being myself
all along if he were in the ocean
in proportion—
but his kind of death made me look
so small standing in it.
Not a very romantic
humiliation, though so easy
into that ocean-abusive, I
sweat, going after him with a rope
until my muscles screw
up and chilly.
Not anywhere was he
himself in focus—
I held that vision tight
so he wouldn't know our distance
My brother stayed wet. I
said he was dead. I said
keep what you love
about the ocean if you can:

our miniature shipwreck
turning on its surface,
the color of milk in a bowl.
Don't swim so far so I can't
see, I said. But he did anyway
and that time I did not lose him.

SEX DRIVE

It isn't suicide. You don't leave
a note. Tulips squeezed
by a red ribbon.

I was human in private. Summer gorging
videos where you exist.

I replay them until they dissolve, proofreading
for accuracy, looking at a landscape so long

it erases itself. My room breaks off the hill
and floats into the night.

Now my body has its own agenda:
moon comma dream comma moon.
No shortage of materials to make me come.

I project one child on top of another,
that summer on top of the other. Home
with the video of home.

I download darkness onto my phone,
the darkness of that summer, its deepest ripple,
and enter my body. You are something
to be drowned in.

I have desires I am not ready for.

GOOD NIGHT'S SLEEP

It takes a long time, at least a good night's sleep, for you to burn
Your ashes snowing in their fancy glass globe in front of us
I take off the solid black dress mother wore to the funeral
when she was my age, too, and never see it again
I shut the door to my room and never come out again
When no one is home, I land into your pile of clothes:
like mid-October, like falling-down-rain why'd you sleep through
I look everywhere I find without my grief being caught
You were my brother Will in the room of boiling trees
to climb up or down, to hold onto as long as I will, which, of
course, is forever and not ever long enough for me to forgive you

ZERO

You were with me at the end of the century in the living room. I swore the world would stop at midnight, that you would be the final minute I would have on Earth. You stayed—afraid of zero; I anchored my bad green eye in your bad brown eye, ready to obey you when the hour chimed. Zero. I thought you stopped time from nowhere. That the breadcrumbs might lead me back here. How didn't I know what would happen to you, which happens to the one you love when you are young, or because of that.

PRIMARY

I need the drowning

I copy my brother's flowers
How else can I tell
him I'm sorry

The tree left the fruit in an odd-number
hour, coherently

Our long flowers went primary in the mixed light:
white-not-transparent

He kept disappearing by reduction
In a squint I could match him to any larger flower which is
    an inaccuracy

I didn't think I needed to tell you—
that it would be a repeating

I am reacting to him where you kiss me

This doesn't mean I can't hear anything else
but water is a distraction

I have no other romantic comparison

VOICE BROKE

my phone died at four o'clock
my hair my lantern died your lawn
mower bright yellow your computer died your heart
your broke lava lamp leaked your ankle
in the slick dark broke summer died the Earth
passed you passed the park where the moon
disappeared your child disappeared in a dream
your childhood appeared you were a child there
swaying on the tree broke the branch died
the treehouse in a dying tree stayed up until you outgrew it
they tore it down you saw them do it your grandfather
fell your favorite tree the clock died at four o'clock
the car broke down the hallway your mother lost
an earring back the heater died the camera
the radio you sang a song at your shoes matched
at your brother's burial your voice broke when you tried
to speak about anything you stood next to the road
waiting for help the trees stopped flashing you birthed
in broad daylight a bright blue baby you died
or you would have died you decided to keep living after
to clean the house to dye your hair back to brown

PART III

ROUGH CUT OF SNOW

CATHEXIS, OR I'VE ALREADY SEEN YOU

We wake in the moon dark, blizzarding, at the same time.

The first ones out in the snow, the morning not even light yet:

a different drawer of light. Leftover night light, laundry glow.

Dream light, milk light, moon upside down not-night.

I've been to another planet, you say. *I've been to this one already.*

This doesn't surprise or upset me. I ask you to tell me more.

For I've felt this before, swapped this memory for one I had
    with my mother

whose dark hair I cannot remember. We were in the middle
    of the road in the snow

in a time neither before or after our separate childhoods
    which sometimes felt like one.

I don't even close my eyes to see it, to feel her next to me. Our
    memories overlap,

both wrong in their specific ways. If I could see how she saw it.

But the snow is the same snow. I am my mother's dark hair.

The whole dream shakes when the first snowplow slows
for us to pass.

Well, I can't tell it from the beginning, you say, *but you were there.*

SOME WOLVES

Our dwelling was fixed with white roses. Our babe a little stem.

I held onto your wrist like someone ran me over in a dream.
All your hair in the bathtub like you were dead.

Wedding or not, I had always loved you deeper, friend.

I will help you move. I will carry your other. I am a sugar pea.
Our love carries itself over the ocean when our son learns to
swim, despite it.

That is some private information—where I will be sleeping
    tonight.
Those are personal pillow patterns: pink peony and American-
    edged girl.

I sway in my desk chair and eat all the apples on the floor
    solemnly. They were
created. After you I have to check my pillowcases if this is real.
    No black sheets. I
am doing all right despite the names of the forests I am lost in.

Some wolves. Some wolves don't look like they will eat you.
    Some
wolves are beautiful and friendless. Some wolves' fathers die
    when
it is just light out. Some take a very long time to move on.

Red trees, the world where we eat together, on our mantle
    encased in snow.

What nothing do I owe you for saving a sliver of my life, for giving me someone to talk to when the wave was coming, when the wave wasn't letting me go.

HOW TO TURN MYSELF OFF

I appear at the glass door of your old apartment with
   groceries.

We are younger here, but not by much. We are childless.
I feel all of the sleep we are about to lose.

It is going to rain soon; we camp out on the storm couch.
After we have sex, I cry anyway, even though we are
together. You stay up until two watching television.

I will dream of you for the rest of my life.
You will dream of me too, but not in the way I want you to.

Now I send myself into the woods to sleep with the first
   man I find.
He lives in this college town, too.
A fog calms the windows of his room. I swirl the dust off the
   books.

I really want to fuck you, I tell him, but I want to be asleep
   forever under
those trees before the winter slams its snow down. To be
   gorgeous like
that, to make all things cold.

He doesn't know I have a baby. Even I forget sometimes.
My body is torn but responds. It will get me through the
dark days of missing you to come.

I love kissing you, the man says. He sings as I pull my
    underwear
back on, tell him to turn around.

But it's you I want. I miss you right here, in this red kitchen.
    I miss
your hands on my shoulders, the way you left your socks
    out in little
piles. And then I keep going.

I've begun taking baths again. I make myself all of my
meals. At the store you helped me buy duplicates of
your knives, your pots and pans.
I want our white shower curtain, I tell you.
Here it is.

Would I fall into your arms? I know I would.
Your garage shoes sit by the door, their heels pressed down
like you're still standing on them.

I think of moving them, and then of how badly
you wanted to die when you were with me.

You said you would just walk into the woods and not come
    back.

This is more peaceful: some other man touching me for an
    hour,
and you alive, watching television in your new apartment a
    half mile from mine.

IN THE SNOW GLOBE WEATHER

In the snow globe weather it is time to move on.
Imagine this house empty, another child conceived in your
     love-
room, the off-white dresser on the snowy curb. Maybe brown
     eyes
this time, maybe a girl.

We never lived here, only followed routine, and
learned the names of each thing we could not see:
snowplows, commotion, birth story.

We broke up here, in every room of the house, against
windows, on the floor. It was our lovemaking, all of that
ending and ending again.

I was teaching our son to spell. I got to the letter O
and I wanted to stop my heart.

I am over the moon's glow
that I can't sleep through.

We begin a long time ago, before Earth, and we are
born randomly out of mothers.

I invented you out of time and we needed each other, only
     briefly—
we will not make any love again on this Earth.

But if we do, I will feel the fake snow and be warm in it.

I DON'T WANT TO BE A SAD MOTHER

The moon looks rough tonight.
I scrape my eyelashes on it. I need a full kiss
in the dark.

This year I sleep with no one on my new pink sheets.

Missing you begins the first time I hold you
in the operating room.

Things are set up in a way
in my heart. I don't want to be a sad
mother.

Already I have used you to comfort me.

Already you have driven me mad—into the icy woods
where I had to imagine waves until I was calm.

Forgive me. I have hated myself since I was a little girl.

When your father leaves me, I can't tell you, so I never do.

When you wonder who loved who more, I can only say
I wanted you more than your father.

SLEEPING APART

In March we made a flower in my belly. We asked why
each other was sad, wondered if we should abort the
flower.

Spring was large; you turned forty, a chocolate birthday cake.

I started collecting miniatures: a pinecone,
a winter sea leaf.

☾

The flower brought us light pain; we slept apart sometimes,
me down the hill from you, my set of porcelain flowered
plates.

You didn't think we would make it.

You cried on the bed, in the kitchen.

You were a beautiful father, I thought. Yours had died when
    you were ten.
Your mother told you he went to live in heaven. Why, you
    wondered, didn't
he want to live with us?

☾

I decided to let the flower grow. You agreed, checked your
    phone.

I waited for you to love me again, as you had.
When you said I was such a good girl in Rowan's room.

Those cold floorboards, our bed on the floor.

Something about the winter before getting pregnant.
We held hands when we slept. We stood on a frozen bridge
   above a frozen river at midnight.

Long before our flower grew it was growing.
My medicine looked like snowdrops; they would fail me.

We drove across Iowa, trees and stars, a gas station in
   Waterloo
with a family in it.
We made love once every day,
At every hour the wet sheets; sometimes you held me long
   after I did not want to be held.

☾

When the flower came, I stayed on our bed. Milk poured
   out of my body.
You listened for my crying in the shower, considered taking
   your own life
once in a while.

I don't like to think about the past, you tell me. But you
   would stay up with me
and pat my belly. I told you what I worried about.

We watched the flowers die in the yard and when I
  checked—rubbed

your black hair, stepped on your back—we still loved each
  other.

☾

When you slept I was awake, when I slept you were awake.
Some days I wish we never kept the flower. Those days I
  think are hell.

And why should I have to think such a thing. Our love ran
  out of water
and who can say if it was the flower or the not the flower.

No more flowers grew in my belly. I no longer need
  medication.

I stopped loving you hard; my desire barely wakes me up.

☾

Tonight you move your bed down the street. I imagine it
  takes you four years,
that you carry it all by yourself back in time to heaven.
Across the plain road, the young trees that will always be as
  far apart in age.

I dream. I say, I don't want you to go. Please don't leave us,
I dream on the floor. Our boy wanders above me into the
  room. He's bringing me a tiny train.

TWO

Bright black bathroom tree, a sale on wool socks.
Special milk in cold metal cups. Unhappiness picks me.
Baths in my son's bathwater while he is at his papa's house.
Organic bubbles. My body is not the body you opened.
I am not what will do. Warm moon, pruned.
I pick my dead-skinned heels. I adore nothing.
Scroll for a twin bedspread covered in blue whales.

Make a list of what you want in a man. I want a man,
I think, who will go on a hike with me. I get drunk off
one glass, like I do. Everything I buy, I buy two.
Every man I sleep with has back problems.
Nerve damage. They have lived long without me. I
text a married man who hears the train just before I do
as it slips out of our town. We should have had one
more kid, I know you agree. We should have it right
now, in fact. I drain the bathtub, eye the mold on the
ledge. Who cares if we are not together.
It would only take half an hour.

PLAYSCAPE

You mutter flower.
You Copenhagen. You snow storms.
You dreamscape. You cheapskate.
You ice cake. You ice skates. You abandon apple.
You space need. You Tinder. You tender her in your arms.
You orange Julius. You caesarian. You dessert menu.
You rip pages. She just comes over, trusts the potted plant.
You hoover; freeway; dead end. You, dead end. Hover a key.
I follow where you cursor. Your hardware store displays
    bleach sinks.
You sleep talk. You repeat my name, the dead one. You
    daydream. Your feet
smell sea-salty. You ooze wine. You feminize a snowstorm.
    You address
your senator. You wing class with aplomb. You tell her she's
    an iceberg. You sway her, OK her.

FOOTNOTE TO A BLIZZARD

Where you sleep, dark snow lashes down. Your glasses are ice-
    cold; your
eyesight astigmatic.

Your sleep, spondaic—a dream of unclogging the sink, of
    missing the toilet, of
breathing without a mask in a party of strangers.

☾

I mistake the snow for a sign, unusually late this winter.
The doctor asks if I have plans for a pregnancy in the next
    twelve months.

Lemons sour on the window ledge; the pines doubled down: I
shudder, turn the coffee on. No, I smile, no plans.

But I should need my womb, like cash just in case.
Imagine I will use it again, to wind it up & listen.

☾

Now, the first snow of December. Corner of a new year;
proper to fill it with something and
shake it out.

The pregnant women line up six feet apart at the clinic, lost in
the forest, their phone screens cracked & low on battery.

☾

The laptop overheats, like it's about to take off. You prefer
other women.

The snow is an afterthought to you, an obstacle to shovel out,
a mass of cells: cancer
or fetus.

☾

I leave myself behind on my walk. This snow walk will be
unlike other snow walks. This
pregnancy will be unlike the other.

I will be a good mother this time, for most of the while.

☾

The moon doesn't move but I have been tracking her with my
eyes for decades, always thinking
I was being followed.

I have a line on my forehead now. I have snow in my boots
already.

Some snow sticks to my eyelash. In the abstract, men are
already out with their shovels.

The moon did this, subjectively.

The thick bend of the spruce, more than three
hundred winters on its back.

☾

This is your sixth winter.

I will walk you through it as you run ahead, your red sled
    already at the steepest
spot of the hill. You are so unlike me most of the time.

Snow is no explanation but I offer it anyway.

I would have another child if it could be you. I would marry
    a man, on
one condition:

MOON CHARGER

We drink night milk with ice chips. We make quick
love. I quiet down with a thumbprint.

I have two lives, I tell you, and you agree.

Now that night comes sooner, my son grows in the bath
like mega-magic-starfish from the dollar store, or the
    staircase is steeper
to his toy-room.

I carry him anyway, a suitcase of stars.

I wear white socks, fluffy socks, identify the tree blooming in
    our windowsill.

I give my son a night bath, watch him play in the yard with
    sticks, the only light a
motion light and the shallow moon, an electrical outlet.

Plug the wrong wire into my computer, the watch charger,
    the phone power.
I stare at my son playing in the dark outside.

He needs privacy now, a notebook with a tiny golden key.

You doctor me. I stare at the painting of my cell phone. Text
    you back
and forth. Swipe blue light, swipe until blue light of morning,
    yolk bright.

Unplug my chargers, let go of each wire. I marvel at my son,
   want another.
Want a dozen others, all sleeping tangled, and the ocean—
   chilled and chilly.

Go to the doctor, spread my legs. Fill up the gas tank with
   diesel, boiled
lemon in my tea, sea salt on my soft egg. Start the oven timer.
I cook an ocean fish, a lake fish, a wild animal.

I look you in the eyes and say let's start over.

INTRODUCTION TO FLOATING

In the short history of night, you ride your bike like
a horse, a telephone in your pocket.

I book you, indefinitely, for the stars, for the sight of you
    ahead on the
winding trail, my ear up to the abalone.

I step from my house into yours through the icy dark, with
    offerings, an
error in a bottle. The cake so sweet, I am allergic.

The foamy sky unloads its opinions, its bluish wind.
Clocks are merely decorative. When you hold me, I
instantly fall asleep, a slogan of rain.

I come like a mother comes, facedown. I curl each hair into
    a wire, halve
the sugar, choose the wrong egg, the bloody one.
I have another son in me, by default, by midnight.

Spines of evergreens press into my back, how darkness
    blushes the
videotapes of home—I hear a waterfall.

There used to be a house on that hill, slanted by the salted
    ocean.
I was that house, inches from flooding, basement steeped in
    groundwater.

Plants grasp and gather to the light. A forest is inside you.

As you were, sailing. As you were, gasping at a bright yellow
  leaf I almost step on.
I listen to the rain on the roof like a guest telling me her
  address.

FORCE MAJEURE

Night and I open
in the milky dark, clotted
with stars. I refuse
to let die my parents, especially
both of them.
Winter unloading
the dishwasher without
going insane.
Downstairs the dryer
rattling a shark tooth
in a coat pocket.
I have wasted your childhood,
photographed you too much.
Above the kitchen
sink, fluorescent snow
makes the cold bearable.
I frost two layers of yellow
cake, lick the whisk absently.
You assure me you will find
me in the next life,
and the one after, that no other
mother will do.
Bored, I gave birth out of my birth
canal like it was nothing.
I can never leave you now.

LONELIEST DAY OF BEING YOUR MOTHER

Even now, your not loving is
all I have to go on

Your not loving as heavy as nights the winds blow
the trees down and they are up again by morning,
shaking with light

Most mornings I am looking for the damage on the road
from my house to your father's house. The distance is
small but important, lined with cranberry clusters

Loneliest day of being your mother is not being
with you. Loneliest day the light in your room
fading your primrose blanket

The softest thing in the house, the oldest, and
most dead. Being a mother is touching your soft
skin when you are not here, collecting shelves of
books, growing evergreens

At the beach I wait for your kite to come down.
I will tell you your birth was a song and nothing else,
not that you almost killed me, because you didn't

I am not a toy swimming in the wide open sea. I
cannot be made love to. I cannot love anything except
when it's yours

LAST OF

Around our village is a body of water

If it didn't get killed in winter, it comes back with
color

My mother put her head in the lake to relax

I visualized her pain as a mass of black stars
floating around her, making her healthy or
unhealthy, asleep or awake

While we kept growing, she seemed to get smaller, headache or
no headache, I never thought I could keep her

I pulled off the blanket to look at her bruise, as real as
her room on the edge of the house, as secret

When I burned this story down, incidentally, her
sweater I found at the bottom of the black lake,
handpicked

If you are missing, you exist

BABY DOLL

I tried your death
out

but I couldn't, not to
sink in the lake

of my dark blue
body

My heart stayed the same
size

Yours grew
milk

I used to sleep. Now, I lie
very still—

the lake so blue
it's black

I can't leave my body
here:

You will think
my death

is a drink to
drink

WHERE YOU GET YOUR
DISTANCE FROM

I turn my back to the pines. No matter where I hang the calendar
it looks wrong, paused on October.

I am grown. I have painted and repainted my dining room to get
the yellow out. The flowers absorb it, alive longer than usual.

Tiny ripples in my thighs when you squeeze me.
I am dead landscape in your left arm.

I almost married no one. Almost gave birth to no one.
I kept waiting to be myself in this town. I bought a house and a
    treehouse.

The rain looks painted onto my sheets.
The world bends over. We wake in the morning and it is so bright.
I sleep well here, you say.

With these antidepressants I barely need sex; I barely need the
    acorns
off the trees, but I want them.

I sit in the tub after I drop my child off at his father's new
apartment, relieved no one loves me romantically.

SLANTING SNOW

You were surprised it was winter in heaven, too, that
you knew no loved one under all that slanting snow

You followed the hooves in the mountain chain until certain the
slaughtered animal was female, before going back to your
    blurry cabin

You had sex with yourself, which warmed you up, even when you
were young, scared to be abused, of having to die in front of your
parents

You had been good enough after all

WOOD THRUSH

I stood in the ice storm that killed the wood thrush & sang to it
But what was haunting me wasn't dead or dying:

At first what you left on Earth had no end point

When I walked into your room, they flew out of my hands:
zeros & ohs, ones & eyes on the telephone keys

Icicles, details of tiring winter, thicken my song
dead in my mouth

Not a signal, or a sign, or a symptom
Just your bird, still after you in the dark, finding me instead

FOSSIL GORGE

The stars are loud tonight. My pink house is blued out
in the summer dark.

The world is over but it keeps going. Grief is a stranger.

I pour in bath salts from the Northwest, trace the raised scar
    tissue
of my caesarian.

I do not teach my son to write. He learns all on his own—
the letters of his name wobbly and uncertain, out of order,
in neon washable marker.

Close your eyes, Mama. He builds me a spaceship out of Legos.
Say something beautiful. More beautiful than when I give you a kiss.

I sign him up for martial arts. When you are old enough,
his father says, I will teach you to defend yourself.

A string of odd weather. A winter that lasts eight months. I
    burn our
coats the first daffodil I see.

We make a spell with the acorns along the lane.
My imagination blanks. Weren't we already underwater,
together, in this very spot?

PASSWORD

The moon is two
dimensional. I defrost the
windshield as I cross the
bridge towards home.
My child passes
through a cloud
on a plane.

STACKARS LILLA BASSE

I lose my footing on the blue trail. A snow is coming.
Your gut goes mute.

A dark painting appears in the stairwell. You identify it with
an app.

Inside spring, the reflection of spring. A book of spells from
the childhood before yours, the mother before yours, standing
at the bathroom mirror in the warm morning light,
wondering if she is expecting you.

Your orchid is blooming, very slowly, for a third time, as your
mother
recovers from a virus, as your father arranges imaging
appointments
of his left heart, as a flower grows inside your sister's stomach.

She will ask you to take care of it one day, and you already
know what you will say.

UNFINISHED OCEAN

I was a mother in the snow, crumpled
under a black coat next to the ocean. That winter I lost

seven hundred hours of sleep. God declined
frost on the pines. I fell down the staircase,
turned two ages.

I stopped being sick a long time ago. But
your illnesses are just beginning, in the
paper basket where you sleep.

Your fever bores me—I dream a thin horse got
by the old gray waves.

You are too small. You could drown in an inch
of stormwater the color of your eye.

My heart beats much slower than yours. Everything but the snow
and my brother has disappeared.

I used his name for you so I could sleep on his floor.
He's smaller than an hour a month.

When I die, I see him walking clearly into the unfinished ocean,
    and even
though I love you, I go with him.

NOTES

"Stackars Lilla Basse" borrows its title from John Bauer's painting.

"Mother Summer" and "Voice Broke" are inspired by Johannes Göransson.

The line "I am making a film" in "Does Monogamy Suit You" is in response to Jonas Mekas.

"Death By Landscape" borrows its title from Margaret Atwood's story.

"University of Iowa Hospitals & Clinics" is inspired by Tomaž Šalamun.

"Sugar" is in response to Anne Sexton's "Hansel and Gretel."

"Force Majeure" borrows its title from the Ruben Östlund film.

The line "zeros & ohs, ones & eyes on the telephone keys" in "Wood Thrush" is inspired by Vladimir Nabokov's story "Signs & Symbols."

ACKNOWLEDGMENTS

Thank you to the editors of the following journals in which some of these poems originally appeared:

The Adroit Journal: "Eggs After Sell-By Date" and "Drift"

Bear Review: "Offspring"

Best American Poetry 2022: "Myths About Trees" (originally in *West Branch*)

Bennington Review: "University of Iowa Hospitals & Clinics" and "Treatment"

BLAAAH Magazine: "Good Night's Sleep"

Brink: "Video Footage," "Where You Get Your Distance From," and "Two"

B O D Y: "Unfinished Ocean" and "The Middle House"

COUNTERCLOCK: "Moon Charger"

The Columbia Review: "Playscape"

The Cortland Review: "In the Snow Globe Weather"

Day One: "In Proportion"

EX/POST: "Death by Landscape"

Handsome (Black Ocean): "At the Lake" and "Sketch of Winter"

HOW Journal: "Last of"

The Hopkins Review: "Voice Broke," "Mother Summer," and "Does Monogamy Suit You"

The Iowa Review: "At Squire Point" and "I Don't Want To Be a Sad Mother"

The Journal: "Sugar" and "Wood Thrush"

Juxtaprose: "The Field"

Los Angeles Review of Books: "Katarina"

Leveler: "Sleep Anxiety"

Narrative Magazine: "Force Majeure" and "Introduction to Floating"

North American Poetry Review: "Visitor"

Pangyrus: "Dispatch"

Pacifica Literary Review: "Owl"

Prairie Schooner: "How to Turn Myself Off" and "Sleeping Apart"

Phantom Limb: "Invitation From My Brother"

Ploughshares: "A Disease of the Mind"

Stone Canoe: "Slanting Snow"

Spoon River Poetry Review: "Loneliest Day of Being Your Mother"

Tupelo Quarterly: "Stackars Lilla Basse" and "Footnote to a Blizzard"

West Branch: "Myths About Trees," "Alouette," "Hammerhead," and "Some Wolves"

Yo! New York: "Zero"

This work was generously supported by fellowships from Yaddo and the University of Iowa.

Thank you to Karen Craigo and Michael Czyzniejewski at Moon City Press for choosing this book and for your guidance. It is a dream come true.

To my teachers, especially Mark Levine, James Galvin, Reginald McKnight, Dora Malech, Ed Pavlic, and Arda Collins. Thank you for your mentorship and for encouraging my voice.

Thank you, Sabrina Orah Mark, for making my life as a writer possible. And thank you to Andrew Zawacki for the continued conversation over the years and detailed notes on the manuscript.

Thank you to my friends and fellow writers for their support, especially Hélène Sicard-Cowan, Dan Kraines, Megan Fernandes, Christa Fraser, Carlie Hoffman,

Tina Lemburg Jones, Jessica Laser, Elizabeth Metzger, Caitlin Roach, Heather Sommer, Brittany Siler Sinnott, and Rachel Yoder.

Thank you especially to Hannah Bonner for your friendship and encouragement in everything.

To Andrés Carlstein, thank you for the day-to-day and for being a wonderful father to Félix.

Thank you to Clayton, Marjorie, and Drew Pond, my second family. My childhood was richer because of your generosity and love.

Especially and always, thank you to Stephen Voyce for letting me be myself and for loving me. You are my home.

For my siblings, Laura and John, thank you for all of the joy and for being my anchor. And for Will, whose life inspired these poems and in whose memory all of my work is dedicated. I remember you.

For my mother, Myra, and my father, Glen, for thinking I had a book in me: Mom, thank you for teaching me to see the magic in everything, and Dad, thank you for your gentleness and for giving us the world.

To my son, Félix William: You are my favorite poem and the greatest gift of my life.

And finally, this book is for Catherine Pond, my double, who read every draft over the years. Thank you for carrying me. All of these poems are for and because of you.

Here, the fish are still just forming. The first forests, taking shape.

MOON CITY PRESS
POETRY AWARD WINNERS

2014
Sarah Freligh
Sad Math

2015
Jeannine Hall Gailey
Field Guide to the End of the World

2016
Kerri French
Every Room in the Body

2017
Clayton Adam Clark
Finitude of Skin

2018
Kathy Goodkin
Crybaby Bridge

2019
Bret Shepard
Place Where Presence Was

2020
Claudia Putnam
The Land of Stone and River

2021
Adam Scheffler
Heartworm

2022
Julia Anna Morrison
Long Exposure

Printed in the USA
CPSIA information can be obtained
at www.ICGtesting.com
JSHW022241171123
52029JS00003B/23

9 780913 785775